In the Kitchen with Bob

Light & Easy

IN THE KITCHEN WITH BOB

Light &

Easy

Bob Bowersox

Food photographs by Mark Thomas Studio

QVC PUBLISHING, INC.

QVC Publishing, Inc.
Jill Cohen, Vice President and Publisher
Ellen Bruzelius, General Manager
Sarah Butterworth, Editorial Director
Cassandra Reynolds, Executive Assistant

Produced in association with Patrick Filley Associates, Inc.
Design by Joel Avirom and Jason Snyder
Photography by Mark Thomas Studio
Prop styling by Nancy Micklin
Food Styling by Ann Disrude

Q Publishing and colophon are trademarks of QVC Publishing, Inc.

Published by QVC Publishing, Inc., 50 Main Street, Mt. Kisco, New York 10549

Manufactured in Hong Kong

ISBN: 1-928998-01-1

First Edition

10 9 8 7 6 5 4 3 2 1

Contents

Introduction

Believe it or not, this would have been a difficult book for me to write until a few years ago. You see, "light and easy" was a foreign concept to me until I reached my mid-thirties—you might as well have been speaking Russian to me.

This is mostly due to the fact that my mother and father never put a plate in front of me that didn't have at least three food groups on it, each group a virtual meal in itself. They believed in the power of good food. The more, the better was the way they looked at it. I also think there was a bit of the Reverend Hixon Tracey Bowersox's (my grandfather) axiom that we "should be thankful for our bounty and not disrespect God's gift to us, so sit down and eat."

The upshot was that I grew up believing that you filled the plates to overflowing, and that the heavier the dish, the more probable it was that it contained everything you needed, physically and spiritually.

It wasn't until I hit middle age that I started to explore other possibilities. Lifestyles had changed by then, as had beliefs about food in general. New research on our diets was teaching us about better, healthier eating. What and how we ate became as important as what we breathed. Old ways gave way to new ones.

So I started to look for some new things to put on my table. I wasn't rejecting what I grew up with, I was just looking for new ways to enhance it, evolve it, add to it. But I wouldn't—I couldn't—stomach the tasteless, "low-fat" concoctions that have inundated Americans for the last several years.

Light & Easy is the result of my efforts. And believe me, it isn't diet food. Lighter eating doesn't have to mean deprivation. It doesn't have to involve will power, obscure ingredients, difficult culinary techniques, or strange balances of proteins and carbohydrates. For the most part, it's just common sense, fresh ingredients and a little creativity. And for me, taste. First and foremost, lighter eating has to be tasteful eating. If not, why bother, right?

And while these recipes yield great dishes, they are also very easy to master. You won't have to attend a culinary school to make them. If you can handle a knife, a spoon, a whisk, and maybe a blender or food processor at the most, then you know everything you'll need to know. And nothing here will take you very long—I've gone light and easy on the time needed, too.

The recipes are grouped for today's living, as well. Many times we try to lose a little weight, go a little lighter, by dropping a meal a day, or limiting our intake during a specific time of the day. But that often results in our overeating at other times of the day. Current research actually tells us that it's better to have four to six smaller meals throughout the day—spreading out our intake—than it is to skip a meal and overeat later. So I've included recipes for each of the main eating times in our modern-day lives, to help you wisely and healthfully manage your meals.

I've started you out with a section on Breakfast & Snacks. My folks always told me that it was the most important meal of the day, and I've never been able to prove them wrong—if I don't get a good breakfast, I just don't work as well through the day. But a good, energizing, tasty breakfast doesn't have to be grease and fat laden. Some mid-morning or mid-afternoon snacks are included in this section, as well. These light yet satisfying ideas will take the edge off your hunger and satisfy your sweet tooth at the same time.

The Lunch section will delight you with light and easy ideas that can be made quickly in the middle of a busy day, or made in advance and taken easily to work. Being a big lover of unusual salads (what's more boring and tasteless than iceberg lettuce and a couple of tomatoes? No wonder we smother that kind of salad with fatty dressings!), I've included many creative ideas here, including soups and delicious pocket sandwiches.

Dinners are always the tough ones to keep light and easy and still flavorful and substantial. In Weekday Dinner you'll find a little bit of something for every palate, from burgers, seafood and pasta, to fajitas, stir-fry and pizza. But they all can be made in minutes, and each one has its own special "something" that will make it a standout without weighing you down.

Sometimes, however, what we serve ourselves and our families during the week is not as fancy as we'd like it to be when we entertain guests. But we don't have to forego the light and easy approach just to make such meals a notch above. I've included a special Entertaining section just for those times when something special is needed, but you want to leave out the hassle and the heaviness.

Finally, Desserts. And sticking "light and easy" in front of the word "dessert" is not necessarily an oxymoron. Just because you want a sweet, tantalizing finish to a fine meal doesn't mean you have to accept a plateful of calories and fat. Just wait 'til you try a few of the recipes in this section!

In conclusion, let me assure you that I'm not standing on a soapbox here, shouting the dangers of the modern American diet. Heaven knows I eat my share of creamy sauces and rich desserts. Nor am I trying to tell you that using these recipes exclusively will do anything other than change what you're currently eating. But one other thing I remember my mom and dad, and especially the Reverend Hixon Tracey telling me —"All things in moderation."

Perhaps that's the best advice of all. Enjoy the variety of the bounty we are blessed with in America. A little of this, a little of that. And if you can work in a few *Light & Easy* recipes, so much the better. Enjoy!

BREAKFAST & SNACKS

Apple and Cranberry Cake

MAKES 12 SQUARES

THERE'S NOTHING QUITE LIKE something warm and fruity to set a morning on the right track. Here's a combination of sweet and tangy that can brighten it, as well. Try keeping on hand a plastic container of the first four dry ingredients all sifted together. That will make it much faster for you in the morning. Substitute fresh fruits in season for the cranberries if you'd like, or add chopped nuts to the recipe, though adding the latter will increase the fat in the final dish.

Vegetable spray

1 cup white flour

1 cup whole wheat flour

1 tablespoon baking powder

½ teaspoon salt

½ teaspoon allspice

1 egg

1 egg white

½ cup evaporated skim milk

2 tablespoons corn oil

⅓ cup maple syrup

1 large apple, peeled, cored, diced

½ cup chopped fresh cranberries or ¼ cup dried

Preheat the oven to 350°F. Coat a 9 x 9-inch baking pan with vegetable spray.

In a large bowl, sift together the dry ingredients. In another bowl, combine the remaining ingredients, except for the apple and cranberries. Mix together the wet and dry until just blended. Gently fold in the fruit. Pour the batter into the prepared pan and bake for 25 to 30 minutes. Remove from the oven and allow to cool in its pan for 10 minutes before cutting into squares.

NOTE: These can also be made as muffins. They freeze well, too.

Pumpkin Muffins

THESE ARE NOT JUST for late fall mornings. They're great to keep on hand all year. They're quick and easy to make, and they last in the freezer for about a month, making it easy to grab one, toss it in the microwave for a minute or so, and head out the door.

Preheat the oven to 400°F. Coat a muffin tin (with 2 ½-inch cups) with vegetable spray. In a large bowl, sift together the next 5 ingredients. Stir in the oatmeal. In another bowl, beat the wet ingredients. Combine the wet and dry and pour into the prepared muffin tins. Bake for 20 to 25 minutes. Allow to cool for 5 minutes in the tins and then remove to a cooling rack.

Vegetable spray
¾ cup all-purpose flour
¼ cup whole wheat flour
1 tablespoon baking powder
½ teaspoon salt
¼ teaspoon ground mace
¾ cup uncooked instant oatmeal
1 egg
1 egg white
1 cup canned pumpkin puree
½ cup nonfat plain yogurt
2 tablespoons corn oil
¼ cup maple syrup

Banana Muffins

MAKES 12 MUFFINS

My father always made banana bread—it was one of his favorites. Here's a quick and easy way to get the same great flavors without having to go through the work of making bread. It's also an excellent way to make use of bananas that have gotten a little too ripe for other uses—in fact, the riper they are, the sweeter the muffins. Like the Pumpkin Muffins on page 11, they also freeze well for keeping on hand.

Vegetable spray

½ cup all-purpose flour

½ cup whole wheat flour

½ teaspoon baking soda

1 teaspoon baking powder

½ teaspoon salt

½ teaspoon ground cinnamon

¼ teaspoon ground nutmeg or freshly grated

1 cup uncooked instant oatmeal

1 egg white

1 egg

¼ cup maple syrup

2 tablespoons canola oil

2 ripe bananas, mashed

½ cup vanilla yogurt

Preheat the oven to 400°F. Place 2½-inch muffin cups in a muffin tin and coat the inside of them with vegetable spray.

In a large bowl, sift together the flours, baking soda, baking powder, salt, cinnamon and nutmeg. Stir in the oatmeal.

In a medium-size bowl, whisk the egg white until it is foamy. Add the remaining ingredients. Fold the wet ingredients into the dry until just combined.

Spoon the batter into the prepared cups and bake for about 25 minutes, or until a toothpick inserted into the middle of a muffin comes out clean. Allow the muffins to cool in the tin.

Blueberry Yogurt Pancakes

MAKES ABOUT 12 PANCAKES

ASK MY DAUGHTER TAYLOR what she wants for breakfast, and the answer's always the same—"Blueberry pancakes!" And while I indulge her whenever possible, I'm also trying to keep her eating healthy without spending forever doing it. So these 'cakes are perfect for both of us. Feel free to substitute your own favorite fruits for the blueberries—like strawberries or raspberries—as they come into season.

1	cup flour
1	tablespoon sugar
½	teaspoon baking powder
1	teaspoon baking soda
½	teaspoon salt
⅛	teaspoon ground nutmeg or freshly grated
1	egg
½	cup nonfat plain yogurt
½	cup nonfat milk
1	tablespoon vegetable oil
	Vegetable spray
¾	cup fresh or frozen blueberries
	Dollop nonfat vanilla yogurt or nonfat sour cream
	Maple syrup

Stir together the flour, sugar, baking powder, baking soda, salt and nutmeg. In a separate, large bowl, beat the egg with the plain yogurt and milk. Beat in the oil, then add the flour mixture. Stir until just combined (lumps are all right).

Spray a griddle with vegetable spray and place over medium heat until a few drops of water dance on the surface. For each pancake pour about ¼ cup of batter onto the griddle, then sprinkle in a few blueberries.

Cook pancakes on one side until puffy and full of bubbles, then flip and cook on the other. Serve with a dollop of yogurt and maple syrup.

Variations

APPLE PANCAKES: Instead of the berries, fold 1 peeled and thinly sliced Red Delicious apple into the batter.

VEGETABLE PANCAKES: For brunch-type pancakes, replace the berries with ½ small carrot, finely julienned, and ½ rib of celery, finely julienned.

WHOLE WHEAT PANCAKES: To increase the fiber in the pancakes, replace ⅓ cup of the flour with whole wheat flour.

Warm Marmalade Pears

THIS IS ONE OF THOSE bed-and-breakfast dishes that you find in the dining room when you come downstairs in the morning. For all its elegance, it's really quite simple to make. Try it as a personal indulgence some morning, and keep it in mind as an unusual and healthy addition to a brunch buffet.

1   24-ounce can pears, drained

4   ounces orange marmalade

6   ounces orange juice

4   ounces low-fat sour cream

1   tablespoon orange zest

½   teaspoon ground cinnamon

Place the pears in a microwaveable 8 x 8-inch pan. Combine the marmalade and the orange juice and ladle the mixture over the pears. Microwave the pears on high for 4 minutes or until hot. Remove to 4 small bowls. Stir together the sour cream, orange zest and cinnamon and ladle over the pears.

Don Bowersox's Quick Good Morning Coffee Cake

MAKES 9 3-INCH SQUARES

WHILE DAD LAID CLAIM to this recipe years ago, I'm pretty sure it originated with Alice Anthony, my maternal grandmother's housekeeper and cook in West Virginia. I grew up eating Alice's wonderful cakes, pies and cookies, and this coffee cake has her unmistakable "mark" in its lightness and flavor. If you've always been searching for that special coffee cake you've had somewhere you can't remember, maybe you've just found it.

CAKE

- 1 cup flour
- ½ cup whole wheat flour
- 2½ teaspoons baking powder
- ¾ cup sugar
- ½ teaspoon salt
- 2 tablespoons unsalted butter
- 2 tablespoons canola oil
- 1 egg white
- ½ cup low-fat buttermilk

TOPPING

- 3 tablespoons rolled oats
- ¼ cup maple syrup

FOR CAKE: Preheat the oven to 375°F. Sift the flours, baking powder, sugar and salt together. Cut in the butter and oil a little bit at a time, until the mixture resembles cornmeal. In a separate bowl, whisk the egg white and add the buttermilk. Pour the wet ingredients into the dry and stir until just mixed. Pour into a 9-inch square pan.

FOR TOPPING: Combine ingredients for the topping and spread over the batter. Bake for 20 minutes. Remove from oven and cool on a wire rack.

Breakfast & Snacks

Granola

THESE DAYS, YOU CAN FIND three dozen different versions of "granola" on the supermarket shelves. But I'll wager that none of them will measure up to this one. The recipe was left me by a very special friend years ago, and I've never found its equal in a commercial brand. The secret is in the roasting—you have to watch it carefully and catch it just as the color goes from light brown to dark brown, when it's become crunchy but not burned. A little milk, a little raw sugar...heaven in the morning.

- 4 cups whole oats (such as Quaker)
- 1 cup wheat germ
- ½ cup sesame seeds
- 1 cup roasted soybeans
- 1 cup sunflower seeds
- 1 cup cashew pieces
- 1 cup raisins
- ½ cup vegetable oil
- ½ cup honey (or a little more, if you want it sweeter)
- ½ to 1 teaspoon vanilla extract
  Vegetable oil

Mix all the ingredients except the last together in a large bowl until well blended. With a paper towel, wipe the surface of a large cookie sheet with the vegetable oil.

Spread the mixture on the cookie sheet so that you have just covered the surface. Do this in 2 batches if you need to, so that you don't have too thick a layer on the cookie sheet. Place in a preheated 325°F oven for 15 to 20 minutes, or until the granola has just begun to go from golden to darker brown. Remove immediately and let cool on the sheet placed on wire racks until it becomes crunchy.

Store in a resealable plastic bag. Serve with 1% low-fat milk, topped with fruit and raw sugar, if desired.

Breakfast "Power Bars"

MAKES 20 BARS

EVER TAKE A LOOK at what you're paying for the so-called "power bars" in the stores these days? Ever see what's in most of them? Fruits and grains—nature's simplicity. So before you shell out another two, three or four bucks for an 8-ounce bar, whip up a batch of these. They're incredibly easy to make, and are loaded with the whole grains and chewy fruits that make a power bar so satisfying. Make a double batch, so you can keep some fresh in a plastic container, and freeze the rest for later.

Vegetable spray

2 cups uncooked old-fashioned oatmeal

1 cup whole wheat flour

1 cup apple juice concentrate

¼ cup wheat germ

1 cup chopped dried apricots

½ teaspoon ground nutmeg or freshly grated

⅓ cup maple syrup

½ teaspoon salt

½ cup chopped walnuts

¼ cup apricot jam

Preheat the oven to 375°F. Coat a 13 x 9-inch baking pan with vegetable spray. In a large bowl, combine the remaining ingredients, except for the apricot jam, until well blended. Pour into the prepared pan and bake for 30 minutes. Dissolve the apricot jam in a small, heavy saucepan over low heat. Remove the pan from the oven and brush the top with the apricot jam. Cut into bars and allow to cool in the pan before removing.

Tropical Fruit Smoothie

MAKES 4 8-OUNCE GLASSES

HERE'S A HEALTHY WAY to have a non-milkshake milkshake. Smoothies have become enormously popular, and they're quite easy to make at home. This one uses mangoes, which are readily available in the supermarket during the warm months. But you can also use strawberries, if you'd like, or even pears or bananas. Just make sure the fruit is quite ripe, even a little over-ripe.

1	mango, peeled, cut into chunks
1	banana
	Juice of ½ lime
2	cups orange juice
¼	cup honey
¾	cup vanilla yogurt

Place all of the ingredients into a blender and process until smooth.

Creamsicle Smoothie

MAKES 2 12-OUNCE GLASSES

REMEMBER THE FROZEN ORANGE pops filled with vanilla ice cream that you got from the ice cream trucks that came around the neighborhood on summer evenings? This smoothie will take you right back there. Use the juiciest cantaloupe you can find, or let one ripen a few days before using it. These are best with in-season melons. Out-of-season cantaloupes just don't have enough flavor.

2	cups cantaloupe pieces
1	cup orange juice
1	tablespoon honey
¼	teaspoon vanilla extract
1	to 4 ice cubes

Place the first 4 ingredients in a blender and pulse until smooth. Gradually add the ice until the desired thickness is reached.

Breakfast & Snacks

Vanilla Smoothie

MAKES 2 10-OUNCE GLASSES

HERE'S ANOTHER SMOOTHIE IDEA, and one that will especially appeal to lovers of double- and triple-thick shakes. Believe it or not, it's the cottage cheese that really gives this shake its body, and by adjusting the ice cube to cottage cheese ratio, you can change the thickness from light to "impossible to suck through a straw."

½ cup low-fat cottage cheese

2 cups ice cubes

2 tablespoons maple syrup

½ teaspoon salt

1 teaspoon vanilla extract

1 cup vanilla yogurt

In a blender, puree the cottage cheese until it's smooth. Add the ice cubes 1 at a time while the motor is running. When the ice is crushed, add the remaining ingredients and process until well blended. Pour into 2 large glasses.

Mixed Fruit Smoothie

MAKES 1 12-OUNCE GLASS

THIS IS THE ULTIMATE IN A FRUIT SMOOTHIE, and totally customizable as well—substitute blackberries or blueberries for the raspberries, pears for the peaches, or mango for the banana. Makes a great afternoon pause with the Applesauce Spice Cookies on page 26, or either of the muffins on pages 11 and 12.

1 banana, frozen

1 cup frozen peach slices

¼ cup fresh or frozen raspberries

½ cup low-fat vanilla yogurt

1 tablespoon wheat germ

Place all of the ingredients in a blender and pulse until smooth. Pour into a 12-ounce glass.

Pink Lemonade Frappe

During THE DOG DAYS OF SUMMER, *this is a great afternoon drink to cool off with. It can be made with or without the vanilla yogurt, depending on how creamy you'd like it. Pink lemonade also makes excellent frozen pops for kids of all ages (even grown-ups)—the molds can be found in most supermarkets.*

6 ounces pink lemonade
½ cup fresh or frozen strawberries
½ cup low-fat vanilla yogurt
4 ice cubes

Place all of the ingredients in a blender and pulse until smooth. Pour into 2 large glasses.

Nature's Champagne

MAKES 2 8-OUNCE GLASSES

It MAY NOT BE THE BUBBLY *you're thinking of, but it's a great substitute. There's something about the pureed cucumber that spikes up the juices. This is a marvelous way to start a morning, or toast the setting of the sun.*

1 cucumber, peeled, deseeded
10 ounces pineapple juice
2 ounces orange juice

Place the cucumber in a blender. Pulse until it is totally pureed. Add the juices and blend well. Pour into 2 glasses.

Applesauce Spice Cookies

MAKES 24 COOKIES

HERE'S A GREAT COOKIE to spice up that late afternoon break, perhaps with a cup of cappuccino or hot tea. These are not bad as a light dessert with coffee either. They're nice and chewy, with just enough spice to make them tantalizing without being overdone. They freeze well for up to a month but need to be thoroughly defrosted before eating.

½ cup corn oil

1 cup chunky applesauce

½ teaspoon vanilla extract

½ cup whole wheat flour

¼ cup all-purpose flour

¼ teaspoon baking powder

½ teaspoon salt

¼ teaspoon ground mace

¼ teaspoon ground nutmeg or freshly grated

½ teaspoon ground cinnamon

½ cup brown sugar

¼ cup chopped walnuts

2 cups oats

Preheat the oven to 350°F. Mix the wet ingredients in a medium bowl. In a separate bowl, sift together the flours, baking powder, salt and spices. Fold together the wet and dry ingredients. Gradually add the brown sugar, nuts and oats.

Onto a nonstick baking sheet, or a sheet sprayed with vegetable spray, drop tablespoonful-size dollops of the batter. Bake for about 25 minutes. Remove from oven and let cool on a wire rack.

Almond and Jam Thumbprints

MAKES 30 COOKIES

YOU CAN'T GET ANY FASTER than this for cookie making. And the kids will beg you to make them, since they'll get to make the thumbprints! Try making a batch with different fruit jams in the center—choice is always good. If the kids leave you any, you might try them as an elegant, light dessert after lunch or brunch.

2	cups blanched almonds
2	egg whites
2	tablespoons honey
¼	cup all-purpose flour
½	teaspoon salt
1	tablespoon corn oil
¼	teaspoon ground nutmeg or freshly grated
¼	teaspoon ground cardamom
¼	cup fruit jam

Preheat the oven to 350°F. Place all but the jam into a food processor fitted with a steel blade. Pulse until the mixture forms a ball.

Onto a nonstick baking sheet or a sheet coated with vegetable spray, drop teaspoon-size dollops of the dough. With a wet thumb, make an indent in the center of each ball. Into this drop ½ teaspoon of the jam. Bake for about 12 minutes. Cool completely on a wire rack.

LUNCH

Vegetarian Roasted Red Pepper Spread

MAKES ½-CUP SERVING PER SANDWICH

I'M ALWAYS LOOKING for new tastes to put on breads, sandwiches or rolls, or as a topping for meats or vegetables. This one is a beauty, with the sweetness of the red pepper brought out nicely by the roasting and enhanced with the garlic and lemon. Personally, I like things a little hotter than most folks, so I'd add in more Tabasco than specified here. It's great as a base for a grilled vegetable sandwich, or for giving a whole new perspective on a tuna sandwich. You might even want to thin it out with a little olive oil and use it as a coulis with chicken or fish entrées.

1 16-ounce can *white* beans, drained

1 7-ounce jar roasted *red* peppers, well drained

2 garlic cloves, minced

2 tablespoons lemon juice or to *taste*

Dash hot pepper sauce (such as Tabasco) or to taste

2 tablespoons fresh parsley

Salt and freshly ground pepper to taste

Place all of the ingredients in the bowl of a food processor. Pulse until smooth. Adjust the flavors, adding more lemon juice, hot pepper sauce, salt or pepper as desired. Refrigerate for up to 5 days.

Horseradish Coleslaw

SERVES 10

ANYONE WHO KNOWS ME knows how much I love horseradish. Especially hot horseradish. I'm not suggesting you make this one as hot as I'd like it, but anyway it comes, it's a nice change from the usual creamy— and therefore richer in fat—type of coleslaw we're all used to.

2 tablespoons fresh lemon juice

1 tablespoon apple cider vinegar

1 tablespoon extra-virgin olive oil

1 tablespoon prepared white horseradish

1 teaspoon sugar

½ teaspoon freshly ground pepper or to taste

½ teaspoon salt or to taste

¾ pound green cabbage, roughly chopped

1 large carrot

⅛ large red onion, roughly chopped

2 green onions

Personally, I'd use fresh horseradish peeled and chopped in a food processor, or a bottle of "prepared" horseradish—I don't find the creamy horseradish "sauce" flavorful enough.

Whisk together the first 7 ingredients. Using a food processor fitted with a shredding blade, process the cabbage, carrot and red onion. Chop up the green onions and mix all the vegetables together. Toss the slaw with the dressing and adjust the salt and pepper to taste.

Orzo and Red Lentil Salad

SERVES 8

SOUNDS REALLY "HEALTH-FOODY," doesn't it? What if I said "Pasta and Bean Salad"? Because that's really what it is. Orzo is a very fast-cooking pasta that's often neglected, yet is a perfect addition to salads, rice dishes or casseroles. Here we combine it with lentils, a high-protein, low-fat legume that's been cultivated since 6000 B.C. The salad, while quick to make, has a great mixture of textures and tastes, and a gourmet look that will grace any table.

¼	cup orzo
1	cup dried red lentils
2	tablespoons olive oil
1	tablespoon red wine vinegar
1	tablespoon balsamic vinegar
1	garlic clove, minced
½	teaspoon salt
¼	teaspoon freshly ground pepper
2	green onions, chopped
1	cucumber, peeled, deseeded, diced

Boil the orzo in salted water for about 5 minutes, or until tender. Drain and rinse with cold water.

Rinse the lentils and cook them in boiling water for 5 minutes. Drain and rinse with cold water.

Combine the rest of the ingredients and gently toss with the orzo and lentils.

Confetti Potato Salad

SERVES 4

WHAT'S A PICNIC, CHURCH BUFFET or family gathering without potato salad? But who says it has to be the same old thing—dull white and full of fat? This recipe will not only satisfy the requirement for potato salad, but it does it more colorfully and much lower in fat than the "same old, same old." You'll be handling a lot of requests for this one.

6 to 8 medium red bliss potatoes, cut into 1-inch cubes

½ green bell pepper, diced

½ red bell pepper, diced

1 celery rib, diced

3 green onions, sliced

1 tablespoon chopped fresh parsley

1 garlic clove, minced

¾ cup low-fat cottage cheese

½ cup low-fat plain yogurt

1 teaspoon apple juice concentrate

2 tablespoons Dijon-style mustard

1 teaspoon balsamic vinegar

Dash hot pepper sauce (such as Tabasco)

½ teaspoon dried dill

Salt and freshly ground pepper to taste

Steam the potatoes until they are fork tender. Toss them with the vegetables and parsley. In the bowl of a food processor, combine the remaining ingredients and pulse until smooth. Pour the dressing over the potato and vegetable mixture and gently combine.

Quick Vegetable Soup

SHORT ON TIME but you want to put something healthier than canned on the table? Just 15 minutes, and you have a fresh, homemade soup. I grew up with soups like this, watching my mom and grandmom make them from whatever my grandfather brought in from his garden. Believe me— it doesn't take much more time than canned, and it tastes SO much better!

2 teaspoons canola oil

1 teaspoon dried oregano

1 teaspoon dried thyme

1 large onion, coarsely chopped

1 cup coarsely chopped baking potato

1 cup coarsely chopped carrots

1 cup coarsely chopped broccoli

3 cups chicken or vegetable stock

1 bay leaf

Salt and freshly ground pepper to taste

In a large saucepan or stockpot, warm the oil over medium heat. Add the herbs and onion and sauté until the onion begins to soften—3 to 5 minutes. Add all the vegetables, the stock and the bay leaf and bring to a boil. Reduce the heat and simmer until the vegetables are tender—15 to 20 minutes.

Remove the bay leaf, season with salt and pepper and serve.

Quick Gazpacho

THIS IS ONE OF MY FAVORITE SOUPS. In my first book, In the Kitchen with Bob, *I gave you my own favorite recipe for gazpacho. But that version takes a good hour or more to make. So here's a quick, on-the-run version that has all the flavor and gusto that the longer version has, but none of the time requirements. One suggestion: serve it with garlic croutons.*

½	cucumber, peeled, deseeded, diced
½	onion, diced
½	green bell pepper, quartered, seeded, diced
1	large tomato, quartered, seeded
1	garlic clove
1	pimiento
1½	cups tomato juice
2	tablespoons red wine vinegar
1	teaspoon extra-virgin olive oil
½	cup chicken stock
	Hot pepper sauce (such as Tabasco) to taste
	Salt and freshly ground pepper to taste

Set aside a tablespoon of cucumber, onion and green pepper for garnish. Place the remaining cucumber, onion and green pepper, the tomato, garlic and pimiento in a blender and process until smooth. With the motor running, add the tomato juice, vinegar, olive oil, chicken stock, hot pepper sauce and salt and pepper. Pour into serving bowls and garnish with the reserved cucumber, onion and green pepper.

Crab, Cucumber and Radish Salad

SERVES 2 TO 4

IF YOU'RE RUNNING LATE, and the lunch guests are about to arrive, there isn't a quicker, more elegant salad to set before them than this one. Everything about it is simple, except the look and taste. It also makes a great first course for a dinner party. For a variation, substitute balsamic vinegar for the rice wine vinegar.

½ pound fresh crabmeat, drained, picked over

1 small cucumber, peeled, chopped

10 radishes, thinly sliced

½ cup rice wine vinegar

1 green onion (green part only), thinly sliced lengthwise

1 teaspoon sesame seeds

Spread the crabmeat on a platter or in a serving dish. Arrange the cucumber and radishes in layers on top of the crabmeat.

Pour the vinegar over the salad. Scatter the thin strands of green onion over the top, and sprinkle with the sesame seeds.

Mandarin Pitas

SERVES 4

My wife Toni and I like to have "simple" nights, where we don't go to extraordinary lengths to put something interesting on the table. But we still want to make sure that what we serve ourselves and our daughter is healthy and fresh. This dish, which combines what is basically a quick stir-fry recipe with the fun and ease of pitas, is a perfect way to do just that.

2	teaspoons sesame oil
1 ⅓	cups small uncooked shrimp, peeled, deveined
24	snow peas, halved
¼	cup sliced green onions
½	cup sliced water chestnuts
1 ½	tablespoons soy sauce
1	teaspoon grated fresh ginger
½	teaspoon chopped fresh thyme
½	teaspoon chopped fresh basil
4	6-inch pita bread rounds, warmed, top quarter cut off and reserved

In a small skillet or sauté pan, heat the sesame oil over high heat. Add the shrimp and cook for 1 minute. Add the snow peas, green onions, water chestnuts, soy sauce and ginger. Cook 1 minute more. Add the fresh herbs and stir well.

Place the removed top of each pita bread in the bottom of the round to reinforce it. Spoon the shrimp mixture into the warm pita rounds. Serve warm.

Corn Soup with Chives

SERVES 4

HERE'S A RECIPE THAT ACHIEVES *its best during the summer, when corn and tomatoes are at their freshest. But it's not bad in the dead of winter either, using frozen corn kernels. It's so simple, the kids could make it for you, but it has that gourmet restaurant taste.*

A tip for you: When corn is most plentiful, try blanching a batch, cutting off the kernels and freezing them in plastic bags. If you do this, be sure to let the kernels drain until almost dry and then squeeze out as much of the air as possible from the plastic bags. These kernels will keep well in the freezer for a couple of months.

Vegetable spray

2 garlic cloves, minced

3 cups fresh or frozen corn kernels

2½ cups 1% milk

Salt and freshly ground pepper to taste

¼ cup minced fresh chives

1 small tomato, peeled, seeded, diced

Coat a medium-size saucepot with vegetable spray. Over low heat, cook the garlic until it is soft. Add the corn, milk, salt and pepper and raise the heat to medium. Bring to a simmer and cook, stirring occasionally for 5 minutes, until the soup thickens. You may need to mash a few of the kernels against the side of the pot to release some of the starch so the soup will thicken.

Stir in half the chives and simmer 1 minute more. Ladle into shallow bowls and garnish with the diced tomato and remaining chives.

Southwestern Corn Salad Pita Pockets

SERVES 4

EVER WANT TO INTEREST a kid in eating something healthier than a peanut butter and jelly sandwich? As with most anything, the secret's in the packaging. Pita pockets are fun and easily adapted to most anything. This is a marvelous way to serve a salad, and a tray of these, surrounded by grapes, strawberries, melon pieces or whatever fruits are in season, is going to be a hit with kids and grown-ups alike.

In a small bowl, toss together the vegetables. In another bowl, whisk together the next 6 ingredients and pour over the salad. Stuff the salad into the pita halves and top with the bean sprouts.

2 cups corn kernels
½ green bell pepper, diced
2 green onions, sliced
¼ cup sliced cherry tomatoes
1 teaspoon extra-virgin olive oil
1 tablespoon lime juice
⅛ teaspoon ground cumin
1 tablespoon minced fresh cilantro
Dash hot pepper sauce (such as Tabasco)
Salt and freshly ground pepper to taste
2 pita pockets, cut into halves
¼ pound bean sprouts

43

WEEKDAY DINNER

Broiled Portobello
   Mushroom Burgers

Salsa Fish Soup

Baked Fish with Tapenade

Vegetarian Pizza

Stir-Fried Pork
   with Green Onions

Pasta Rapido

Mexican Beef Stir-Fry

Grilled Pork Chops Dijon

Grilled Pesto Chicken

Two-Onion Beef

Tenderloin Tips in
   Garlic Sauce

Spicy Broccoli

Tuna with Tangy Onion Sauce

Quick Shrimp and
   Scallop Cacciatore

Middle Eastern
   Glazed Carrots

Penne Provençale

Turkey Breast Fajitas

Gingered Fennel

Fettuccini with Korean
   Sesame Sauce

"Baked" Potatoes
   with Mock Sour Cream

Beans with Tomatoes

Tuna with Peas and Lettuce

Spinach Rice

Baked Onion Tomatoes

Peppered Salmon

Asian Slaw

Broiled Portobello Mushroom Burgers

SERVES 2

I FIRST CAME TO LOVE portobello mushrooms through my cousin, Tim Wilson. He grilled them one summer evening, topped with olive oil, garlic and shallots. I'd never realized how "meaty" a mushroom they were, and I also fell in love with their dusty, smoky flavor. If you're like me, and you find beef a bit too heavy, particularly on warm summer nights, these burgers might be the perfect substitute for you. They satisfy without the heaviness, and have a fraction of the fat and calories. This recipe can also work for you as a side dish or light entrée, simply by slicing the mushrooms and arranging them over rice.

2   portobello mushroom caps

1   red onion, thickly sliced

2   tablespoons olive oil

1   tablespoon balsamic vinegar

½   teaspoon dried basil

Dash garlic powder

2   hamburger rolls

Brush the under sides of the mushroom caps and the onion slices with the olive oil. Drizzle them with the vinegar. Sprinkle with the basil and garlic powder. In a broiling pan, place the onion slices and mushrooms 6 inches under the flame of the broiler and cook for 5 minutes. Flip them over and cook for an additional 5 minutes. (The mushrooms can also be grilled over medium-high heat for approximately 5 minutes. Turn and cook for an additional 5 minutes.) Toast or warm the rolls. Place the mushrooms and onions on the rolls and pour any cooking juices over them.

Salsa Fish Soup

SERVES 4

Now here's a combination made in heaven for someone like me. Three of my favorite things in one dish. It's sort of like a chowder, but the salsa gives it another dimension—kind of like Boston meets Santa Fe. For the salsa, I might suggest my brother Paul's recipe, which can be found in my most recent book, My Family's Best.

6 cups chicken broth

1 teaspoon salt

2/3 cup regular or quick-cooking rice

2 cups frozen corn kernels

1 pound skinned boned mild-flavored white fish (such as haddock, cod or halibut)

1½ cups mild or hot chunky-style salsa

Lime wedges

In a 5- to 6-quart pan, combine the broth, salt and rice. Bring to a boil over high heat. Reduce heat, cover and simmer until rice is tender to bite—about 15 minutes, or 5 minutes for quick-cooking rice. Add the corn, fish and salsa. Cover and simmer until fish is just opaque at its thickest part (cut to test). Break fish into chunks and ladle soup into 4 bowls. Offer lime wedges to squeeze into soup to taste.

Vegetarian Pizza

I GREW UP ON PIZZA. What kid hasn't? But as I got older and more health-conscious, I stayed away from it, mainly because commercial pizzas always came out dripping with grease and loaded with high-calorie cheeses. But then I met Wolfgang Puck, who showed me that "pizza" is only the canvas—you can paint it any way you like. So here's a pizza for that kid in you who's been aching for a slice. Feel free to add anything else you like...there's no extra charge for additional toppings.

- 1 large pizza crust (such as Boboli) or use your own dough
- ½ cup grated skim mozzarella cheese
- ½ cup grated Fontina cheese
- ½ cup sliced canned artichoke bottoms
- 1 cup sliced zucchini
- 1 cup sliced red onion
- 1 tablespoon grated Parmesan cheese
- 1 teaspoon chopped fresh oregano or ½ teaspoon dried

Preheat the oven to 425°F.

Arrange the ingredients on the pizza crust in the order listed.

Bake for 20 minutes, or until done.

Pasta Rapido

SERVES 4 TO 6

THIS IS, WITHOUT DOUBT, the fastest pasta dish you'll ever make. You don't even have to start the sauce until after the pasta's water is boiling. It's kind of like Provençal aioli, but spiced up a bit with chili peppers. If fettuccini is a bit heavy for you, feel free to try linguini or angel hair pasta. And since it's so quick and easy to make, you might want to try it as a last-minute side dish.

8	ounces fettuccini
2	tablespoons olive oil
2	small dried hot chili peppers, broken into several pieces
2	garlic cloves, minced
½	teaspoon salt
½	cup chopped fresh parsley

Cook the noodles in salted water until just tender.

Heat the oil in a small pan over low heat. Add the chilies and cook until they are brown. Add the garlic and cook for about 30 seconds more, or until garlic is limp. Add the salt and parsley and cook for another minute or so.

Drain the pasta well and place on a warm platter. Pour hot sauce over it and toss gently.

Grilled Pork Chops Dijon

SERVES 2

I LOVE MUSTARD—not the thin, ballpark, yellow stuff, but the heavy, stoneground, Dijon types. And talk about a simple dish! A little quick mixing, a little basting, and you're done. I suggest you bake the chops standing on their bone in a roasting rack, so that as much of the rendered fat and grease as possible just drips off of them and away from the meat. This will require frequent basting with the Dijon sauce, but in the end, it'll be worth the extra effort. By the way, try the sauce as a salad dressing—it's not bad.

1 tablespoon olive oil

1 tablespoon canola oil

¼ cup red wine vinegar

2 tablespoons Dijon-style mustard

1 tablespoon minced chives

1 teaspoon dried tarragon

Freshly ground pepper to taste

2 ¾- to 1-inch-thick loin pork chops

Preheat the grill or oven to 475°F.

In a small bowl, whisk together the oils, vinegar, mustard, chives and tarragon. Season to taste with the pepper. Put the chops on the grill or in a baking dish in the oven. Baste the chops liberally and frequently with the sauce. Cook about 10 to 12 minutes a side, or until done to taste.

Two-Onion Beef

SERVES 4

THIS MAY SOUND LIKE *a good, old American beef dish, but in actuality, it has an Asian sensibility. I do a lot of wokking at home—it's fast and easy—and I came across this recipe a while back. There's a sweet/sour facet to it, but it's the tanginess of the onions that make it a standout. Since you'll want to cook it quickly to keep the sharpness in the dish, make sure you prepare all the ingredients in advance so you can add them quickly as you cook.*

COOKING SAUCE

- 1 tablespoon soy sauce
- 1 tablespoon cornstarch
- ½ cup chicken broth

BEEF

- Vegetable spray
- 1 garlic clove, minced
- ½ teaspoon minced gingerroot
- ¾ pound top round of beef, sliced into ⅛-inch-thick slices
- 1 tablespoon dry Sherry
- 1 tablespoon soy sauce
- 1 tablespoon water
- ¼ teaspoon salt
- ¼ teaspoon sugar
- 1 large onion, cut in half, thinly sliced
- 12 whole green onions, cut into 1½-inch lengths
- Hot cooked rice

FOR SAUCE: Combine the ingredients of the Cooking Sauce in a bowl and stir. Set aside.

FOR BEEF: Coat a wok or wide skillet with vegetable spray and heat over a high flame. When it is hot, add the garlic and ginger and stir once. Add the beef and stir-fry until the meat is browned on the outside, but still pink in the center. Remove the beef from the pan. Deglaze the pan with the Sherry, soy sauce and water. Stir in the salt and sugar. Remove from the pan and reserve.

Stir-fry the onion and add the green onions. Cook for a minute. Return the beef and the Sherry mixture to the pan, add the Cooking Sauce, and heat until the sauce bubbles and thickens. Serve over rice.

Tuna with Tangy Onion Sauce

SERVES 4

My wife Toni and I are Jack Sprat and his wife, for sure. I love fish of all kinds, she's a meat and potatoes girl. But it's not that she won't eat fish...she just hates the taste of it. Even a blander fish like tuna. So I'm always having to come up with a nice sauce to hide any "fishy" flavor she might detect. That's O.K. by me—I love sauces, particularly when they have the word "tangy" associated with them. And as you'll see when you make this, tangy isn't a hard thing to accomplish at all.

1	teaspoon olive oil
1	cup chopped onions
¼	cup red wine vinegar
¼	teaspoon salt
¼	teaspoon freshly ground pepper
½	cup all-purpose flour for dredging
4	4-ounce ¾-inch-thick tuna steaks
2	teaspoons olive oil
	Mint sprigs for garnish

Heat 1 teaspoon of oil in a large, non-stick skillet over medium-high heat. Add the onions and sauté for 5 minutes, or until lightly browned. Add the vinegar, half the salt and half the pepper and cook for 2 minutes, or until most of the liquid evaporates. Remove from the skillet and keep warm.

Combine the flour and remaining salt and pepper in a shallow dish and stir well. Dredge the tuna in the flour mixture. Heat 2 teaspoons of oil in the same skillet over medium heat. Add the tuna and cook for 2 minutes on each side until it is medium-rare, or to your desired degree of doneness.

Serve the tuna topped with the onion sauce and garnished with the mint sprigs.

Penne Provençale

SERVES 3

I WAS INTRODUCED TO THE CUISINE of Provence by Antoine Buterin, one of the top chefs in New York City. I'd met him through QVC, and he invited me to his restaurant in Manhattan. I spent the entire afternoon there, tasting one dish after another, all prepared in the Provence style—fresh vegetables and herbs, clean, tangy sauces, and low-fat and low-calorie contents (which was the most amazing thing, given that it's a French cuisine). I have been in love with it ever since. This is a great marriage of Tuscany and Provence—the pasta and the sauce—and light and quick to boot.

8   ounces pasta (such as penne or fusilli)
1   teaspoon olive oil
1   to 2 garlic cloves
½   large onion, chopped
½   large green bell pepper, seeded, chopped
½   small yellow squash, cut into ½-inch pieces
½   pound ripe plum tomatoes, chopped
    Salt and freshly ground pepper to taste
1   tablespoon garlic breadcrumbs
    Freshly grated Parmesan cheese

Cook the pasta in salted water according to package directions.

In a large, nonstick skillet, heat the oil over medium-high heat. Add the garlic, onion, green pepper and squash. Cook, stirring often, until they are softened. Add the tomatoes and continue to cook until the vegetables are tender. Season with salt and pepper to taste.

Drain the pasta and remove to a serving bowl. Add the vegetables and toss. Serve with garlic breadcrumbs and Parmesan cheese.

Fettuccini with Korean Sesame Sauce

SERVES 4

I ALWAYS LOVE IT when cultures collide—some of the tastiest accidents are the result. Like this dish...part Italian, part Asian, all flavor. While fast and easy to make, it's also amazingly low in calories and cholesterol. My brother-in-law, Ken Morris, a Colorado mountain man by most standards, is a lover of Korean cuisine (he created the Korean Salad I put in my first book). This is a dish he would love. Try it cold as an afternoon salad as well.

1   tablespoon sesame oil

3   tablespoons white vinegar

2   tablespoons hot bean paste

2   tablespoons soy sauce

3   tablespoons sliced green onions

1   garlic clove, minced

1   teaspoon sugar

1   teaspoon freshly ground pepper

2   teaspoons minced fresh ginger

2   tablespoons sesame seeds

12   ounces fettuccini

1   cup frozen peas

1   medium cucumber

While the pasta water is coming to a boil, prepare the sauce. In a bowl, combine the sesame oil, vinegar, bean paste, soy, green onions, garlic, sugar, pepper and ginger. Set aside. Toast the sesame seeds in a large frying pan over medium heat until golden, shaking the pan frequently.

Cook the pasta in salted water according to package directions. Add the frozen peas to the pasta for the last 2 minutes of cooking. Drain and place in a serving bowl. Add the toasted sesame seeds and vinegar mixture and toss well. Garnish with cucumbers.

Tuna with Peas and Lettuce

SERVES 2

In a hurry? It's a way of life around the Bowersox household. So coming up with quick and easy, yet nutritious dishes is a must. My daughter Taylor particularly loves this one (she can relate to the "baby" peas). I personally like the mint and lemon zest in it—they make the whole dish clean and refreshing.

2	cups frozen baby peas, thawed, or fresh
3	tablespoons chopped fresh mint
¼	cup lemon zest
1	garlic clove, minced
3	cups shredded romaine lettuce
2	6- to 7-ounce tuna steaks
2	lemon wedges

In a mixing bowl, combine the peas, mint, lemon, garlic and lettuce. Spread the mixture in a steamer, slightly mounded in the center, so the side steam vents are left open. Place the tuna steaks on top of the center mound. Steam until the fish is opaque and flakes. Transfer the fish to a serving plate, surrounding it with the lettuce and peas mixture. Squeeze lemon wedges over the fish.

Peppered Salmon

SERVES 4

I WASN'T MUCH INTO PEPPER until I married Toni. She's a pepper nut. Whenever we're in a restaurant, the poor waiter is standing there for two minutes grinding pepper onto Toni's salad. But she taught me the difference between freshly ground pepper and the canned ground pepper most of us use. Once I tasted the difference, it wasn't long before I was avidly experimenting with the cooking technique known as au poivre, which means "with pepper." It's so easy to do, and yet the results are spectacular. Try it once. Bet you'll try it again.

1 tablespoon fresh coarsely
ground pepper

4 6-ounce salmon fillets, skinned
Vegetable spray

1 tablespoon sesame oil
Salt to taste

Spread the pepper on a large plate. Press each side of each fillet into the pepper. Grind more pepper if necessary, until all the fillets have been coated with the pepper.

Coat a wide, nonstick skillet with vegetable spray and sesame oil and place over medium-high heat. Add the salmon fillets, side by side, in a single layer, and cook until golden brown on one side. Turn and season with a little salt. Cook until golden brown on the second side, and the fish is starting to flake and is just cooked through. Transfer to serving plates.

Baked Fish with Tapenade

Tapenade has become one of my favorite things (my wife's too, since she loves black olives with a passion approaching fanaticism). It's a Provençal specialty, typically a paste made from black olives, anchovies, capers, and mashed with olive oil and some seasonings like salt and pepper, sometimes garlic. It's usually served as an hors d'oeuvre spread, but in this case, it's a luscious coating that gets baked onto the fish. This is a dish I have no trouble getting Toni, who typically doesn't like fish, to eat.

4 skinless white-fleshed 6- to 7-ounce fish fillets (such as halibut, sea bass, scrod or cod)

Vegetable spray

2 medium tomatoes, cored, sliced ¼-inch thick

1 12-ounce bag frozen peas, thawed

1 8-ounce can pitted ripe black olives, drained

2 garlic cloves

3 tablespoons olive oil

Preheat the oven to 375°F.

Rinse and pat dry the fish. Coat an oven-proof dish with vegetable spray. Place the fish in the dish and surround with the tomatoes and peas. Bake for 15 to 20 minutes, until the fish is just opaque.

While the fish is cooking, in a food processor or blender, process the olives and garlic until finely minced. Add the olive oil in a thin stream; do not overprocess.

Transfer the fish, tomatoes and peas to warm plates and spoon the olive mixture evenly over each fish fillet.

Stir-Fried Pork with Green Onions

SERVES 2

I LOVE SURPRISING MY WIFE Toni and seeing her face light up as she tastes something new and intriguing. This is one of those dishes that can do it. It takes almost no time at all to make, and very few ingredients. Because you're cooking over high heat, you tend not to cook all the flavors out of the ingredients—thus affording you the element of surprise. You'll love the combination of the green onions and garlic—it really dresses up the pork nicely.

½ pound boneless pork loin

1 tablespoon cornstarch

1 tablespoon dry Sherry

    Vegetable spray

1 bunch green onions, cut into slivers

3 garlic cloves, minced

    Salt and freshly ground pepper to taste

Cut the meat across the grain into thin slices, then cut lengthwise into matchstick-size strips. In a small bowl, combine the cornstarch and Sherry. Add the pork to the bowl, stirring to coat well. Marinate for as long as time permits (up to 4 hours).

Coat a wok or frying pan with vegetable spray. Heat over a high flame and add the pork mixture. Cook for 2 to 3 minutes, until lightly browned. Add the green onions and garlic and continue to cook, stirring, for another 2 to 3 minutes. Season with salt and pepper. Serve over rice or in a bowl by itself.

Mexican Beef Stir-Fry

I LOVE GOOD MEXICAN FOOD. Problem is, it's usually loaded with fat and calories (it's all the beef and cheese). Stir-frying, on the other hand, has always been a quick, healthy way of cooking. So by combining Mexican flavors with the Asian technique, we get a weight-watcher's dream—only 229 calories, but loaded with satisfaction.

Vegetable spray

1   pound beef top round steak

1   teaspoon ground cumin

1   teaspoon dried oregano

1   garlic clove, minced

1   red bell pepper, cut into thin strips

1   medium onion, cut into thin wedges

1   to 2 jalapeño peppers, cut into slivers

3   cups sliced romaine lettuce

Coat a nonstick frying pan with vegetable spray. Cut the beef into ⅛-inch strips. Heat the skillet until it is hot. Combine the cumin, oregano and garlic. Stir-fry the red pepper, onion and jalapeño peppers with half of the spice mix for about 2 minutes, until the vegetables are crisp-tender. Remove the vegetables and hold them on a warm plate.

Into the same skillet, add the beef and the remaining spice mix. Stir-fry for 1 to 2 minutes, until the beef is done. Add the vegetables and heat through. Serve over the lettuce.

Grilled Pesto Chicken

SERVES 2

My dad loved pesto. Couldn't get enough of it. He always had a jar sitting in his fridge, and would spread it on crackers or his fresh-made breads. He particularly liked using it as a sauce for pasta (see "Don's Pesto Spaghetti" in My Family's Best, *my most recent book). I've found that a good pesto can be used with just about anything, and is particularly good for sparking up the usually pedestrian boneless chicken breast.*

2   garlic cloves

1   teaspoon salt

2   cups tightly packed fresh basil leaves

2   tablespoons finely chopped pine nuts

2   tablespoons olive oil

2   tablespoons grated Parmesan cheese

2   tablespoons grated Romano cheese

2   boneless skinless 6- to 7-ounce
    chicken breasts

    Salt and freshly ground pepper to taste

This recipe calls for two cloves of garlic, which is O.K., but Dad and I usually put five to six in. But then, we're garlic nuts.

In a food processor or a blender, put the garlic, salt, basil, pine nuts and olive oil. Pulse until smooth. Add the cheeses and process just to combine. The sauce should be spreadable, so add water, if needed.

Lay the chicken breasts on a cutting board and make a slit along the side of each breast. Do not cut all the way through the breast, just make a pocket. Place several teaspoons of the pesto into the pocket and rub the outer surface with some more of the sauce. Season with the salt and pepper.

Place the chicken on a preheated electric grill, barbecue grill or under a broiler and cook until done, about 15 minutes. Serve with extra pesto on the side.

Tenderloin Tips in Garlic Sauce

So often we cook our beef in traditional ways—broil it, bake it, sometimes barbecue it. That's O.K., but I've come to believe we've only gone halfway doing so. I love a good topping or sauce with my beef, and since garlic goes with beef so well, it wasn't hard to see that a good garlic sauce was needed. But sauces are sometimes difficult things to deal with, so it had to be a simple one. Here it is.

1 tablespoon olive oil

8 garlic cloves, coarsely chopped

¾ pound beef tenderloin, cut into 1-inch cubes

Salt to taste

2 tablespoons dry Sherry

2 tablespoons water

Heat the oil in a nonstick skillet until it's very hot. Add the garlic and meat cubes and stir-fry until the beef is brown and done as desired. Season with salt and transfer the meat to a serving dish.

Deglaze the pan with the Sherry and water, loosening any brown bits. Pour over meat.

Quick Shrimp and Scallop Cacciatore

SERVES 4

I HAVE ALWAYS LOVED SHRIMP. I have always loved scallops. But I didn't know from cacciatore until I married Toni (whose maiden name was Parisi). So, in keeping with the truest sense of marriage, we melded everything together. Thus, you get to enjoy a terrific mix of seafood and sauce that, while true to an Italian girl's heritage, can be made within the confines of a busy household's demands. You can also substitute chicken or veal into this recipe as well.

Vegetable spray

¾ pound medium or large shrimp, peeled, deveined

½ pound bay scallops, rinsed

½ cup chopped onion

1 medium green bell pepper, seeded, chopped

1 28-ounce can whole tomatoes, with liquid

1 8-ounce can tomato sauce

½ teaspoon dried basil

1½ cups quick-cooking rice

Spray a medium-size, nonstick saucepan with vegetable spray. Sauté the shrimp, scallops, onion and green pepper for 2 minutes over high heat, stirring constantly. Add the tomatoes, sauce and basil. Bring to a boil.

Stir in the rice. Cover and remove from the heat. Let stand for 5 minutes before serving.

Turkey Breast Fajitas

SERVES 4

THIS IS A LIGHT, QUICK and healthy version of Mexican fajitas. My wife Toni and I started using turkey instead of beef in a lot of our dishes quite a while ago, and have been very pleased with the results. It's a nice summer evening meal, and kids will especially love the "fingers allowed" part of making their own.

1½ pounds turkey breast, cut into strips

3 garlic cloves, minced

2 tablespoons lime juice

1 teaspoon chili powder

1 green bell pepper

1 red bell pepper

1 onion

Vegetable spray

4 to 6 flour tortillas

Combine the turkey breast, garlic, lime juice and chili powder. Cover and refrigerate for 15 minutes. While the turkey is marinating, slice the peppers and onion into thin strips.

Coat a nonstick sauté pan with vegetable spray. Pat the turkey dry. Over high heat, sauté the turkey until it begins to brown—about 5 to 7 minutes. Stir and add the vegetables. Cook for about 5 minutes, or until the turkey is cooked through and the vegetables are limp.

Set aside the filling. Wipe out the sauté pan and heat the tortillas until warmed through. Place about ½ cup of filling in the center of each tortilla and roll up. Serve immediately.

"Baked" Potatoes with Mock Sour Cream

SERVES 2

BOY, DID MY MOM LOVE sour cream! Whenever we had baked potatoes, whether at home or at a restaurant, there was more sour cream on the potato than there was potato. She paid for it, of course—she had a weight problem and high cholesterol, but if you're a lover of sour cream, like Mom, you probably accept the trade off. Well, you don't have to. This is an acceptable substitute, and it can be spiced up with things like a teaspoon of horseradish or Dijon-style mustard, if you wish.

2 large baking potatoes (Idaho are best)

1 cup low-fat cottage cheese

1 cup nonfat yogurt

1 tablespoon minced green onion

Prick the outside of the potatoes with a fork. Microwave on high for 3 minutes. Turn over the potatoes and cook on high for an additional 2 minutes. (If you have time and your traditional oven is on, place the potatoes in it for up to another 20 minutes and a nice crust will continue to develop.)

Place the cottage cheese and yogurt in a blender and process until smooth. Fold in the green onions and serve along with the potatoes.

Spinach Rice

I'LL EAT RICE ANYTIME, anywhere. I got into it during my lean musician days, when all we had to eat every night was some brown rice. But the band and I learned a hundred different ways to sparkle up a bland rice dish, so it was never a problem. This is one of the easy and quick ways we found to bring good ol' rice to a gourmet dinner. It's a perfect match for almost any entrée.

5 ounces frozen chopped spinach, thawed, drained

½ small onion, chopped

2 green onions, chopped

1 tablespoon minced fresh parsley

¼ teaspoon freshly ground pepper

Pinch ground red pepper

¼ teaspoon ground ginger

Salt to taste

1 cup quick-cooking rice

2 tablespoons dry Sherry

2 cups water

In a large saucepot, combine all of the ingredients, cover and bring to a boil. When it comes to a boil, cook for 2 minutes and then remove from the heat and allow to steam for 5 minutes, until the rice is soft and the onion translucent.

Asian Slaw

As I've mentioned elsewhere in this book, by brother-in-law, Ken Morris, is a landlocked Coloradan with his soul firmly placed in Asia. His favorite cuisine is Thai, and he's sent me more good recipes than almost anyone I know. Here's a wonderful twist on regular, old coleslaw, and, if you'd like, you can use more exotic Asian cabbages instead of the plain white that we normally use. Asian cabbages tend to be more delicate in texture and have a slightly different flavor.

- 4 ounces white cabbage
- 2 small carrots
- 3 green onions, thinly sliced
- 1 tablespoon sesame seeds
- 2 garlic cloves, minced
- 1 tablespoon grated fresh ginger
- 1 tablespoon sesame oil
- ¼ cup corn oil
- ¼ cup soy sauce

In a food processor fitted with the slicing disk, run through the cabbage and carrots. Remove to a large bowl. Add the green onions. Sprinkle with the sesame seeds. In a small bowl, whisk together the garlic, ginger, sesame oil, corn oil and soy sauce. Pour over the vegetables and toss well.

Spicy Broccoli

SERVES 4

A RECENT MEDICAL REPORT praised the health benefits of broccoli, especially in the areas of cancer prevention. I've always loved it, but never did much more than steam it. Here's a nice way to bring a quick, easy and healthy side dish to the table, with the hope that with more interesting preparations, we'll all eat a little more of the healthy plant.

⅓ cup currants

¼ cup hot water

1 head broccoli

1 cup orange juice

½ teaspoon ground cinnamon

1 teaspoon ground cumin

   Pinch of cayenne pepper

   Salt and freshly ground pepper to taste

½ teaspoon cornstarch

Place the currants in the hot water while preparing the recipe.

Cut up the broccoli into florets. Peel off the tough outer layer of the stalks and cut into 2 x ½-inch sticks.

In a medium saucepot, place the broccoli sticks and cover them with an inch of cold water. Cover the pot and bring to a boil.

In a separate, medium-size bowl, combine the orange juice, spices and cornstarch and stir until the cornstarch is dissolved.

When the broccoli sticks have come to a boil, add the currants and the orange juice mixture. Stir until it returns to a boil. Add the florets and cover, steaming until the broccoli is bright green and tender. Remove the broccoli to a serving bowl and pour the cooking liquid over it.

Middle Eastern Glazed Carrots

SERVES 6

I GREW UP WITH GLAZED CARROTS. Mom would put them on the table at least three times a week. Hers had a wonderful sweetness to them. This recipe, however, adds some interesting spices to that sweetness, and I think you'll find them appealing to both children and adults. What's also nice is that the entire recipe can be prepared in advance and cooked at the last minute.

1 tablespoon cornstarch

1 16-ounce can ginger ale

1 pound carrots

1 teaspoon ground cumin

½ teaspoon ground cardamom

1 tablespoon chopped fresh cilantro

½ teaspoon salt

In a medium-size saucepot, combine the cornstarch and ginger ale. Stir until the cornstarch is dissolved.

Peel and cut the carrots into 2-inch sticks, or on a bias. Place in the saucepot. Add the cumin and cardamom and bring to a boil. Cook until the ginger ale has reduced to a syrup and the carrots are bright orange and tender.

Place the carrots in a serving bowl, sprinkle with the cilantro and season with salt.

Gingered Fennel

SERVES 6

I'VE OFTEN FOUND that it's the side dishes that can set an entire meal apart, regardless of how exotic or interesting the entrée is. The unusual combination of the fennel's licorice flavor with the pungency of the garlic makes this a side dish that can liven up even the simplest of entrées.

2 fennel bulbs

½ cup chicken stock

½ teaspoon cornstarch

2 garlic cloves, minced

2 tablespoons grated fresh ginger

1 tablespoon soy sauce

Trim the bottom and top stalks off the fennel. Cut the bulb in half and then across the grain into ½-inch slices.

In a medium-size saucepot, place all of the ingredients except the soy sauce. Cover and bring to a boil, stirring occasionally, until the fennel is tender, about 10 minutes. Remove the fennel to a serving bowl and sprinkle with the soy sauce. Toss well.

Beans with Tomatoes

SERVES 6

COLORFUL IS THE NAME of the game here. I've been told by those who know best that 75% of the reason we like a meal is the presentation—the mix of colors and textures, the balance on the plate, etc. Well, if you're looking to add color, this recipe's a beauty. It's a quick and easy way to add something a bit more interesting to your plates.

1 pound tomatoes

Vegetable spray

1 shallot, finely chopped

1 garlic clove, minced

Salt and freshly ground pepper to taste

8 ounces green beans, trimmed, cut into 1 ½-inch pieces

2 tablespoons chopped fresh basil

Bring a small pot of water to a boil. Cut out the black eye (where the stem attaches) of each tomato. Slash an X on the bottom of each. Drop the tomatoes into the water for 30 seconds. Remove the tomatoes with a slotted spoon and rinse with cold water. Remove the peels, cut each one in half and poke out the seeds. Coarsely chop each tomato.

Coat a large saucepan with vegetable spray and heat over a medium flame. Add the shallot and garlic. Cook for 2 to 3 minutes. Add the chopped tomatoes and cook for about 10 minutes, until the water evaporates and the tomatoes are soft. Season with salt and pepper to taste.

While the tomatoes are cooking, bring a pot of salted water to a boil. Add the beans and cook for 4 to 6 minutes, or until tender. Drain, stir into the tomato mixture, add the basil and cook for another 2 minutes.

Baked Onion Tomatoes

I LIKE STUFFED TOMATOES. They're a great side dish, they're easy to prepare and they're not fussy—they can usually be baked right alongside of whatever else is in the oven. Temperature doesn't really matter to them. While the green onions indicated here give the stuffing a zinginess, you can also add in garlic, shallots, mushrooms, bell peppers—whatever you fancy at the time.

4 tomatoes

4 green onions

¼ cup fresh breadcrumbs

½ teaspoon salt

   Freshly ground pepper to taste

   Extra-virgin olive oil for drizzling

Preheat the oven to 350°F.

Using a small knife, cut the tops off the tomatoes. (Dice and use in a salad.) With a spoon, scoop out about a tablespoon of the insides of each tomato.

Finely chop the white ends of the green onions and divide into the well of each tomato. Chop up the green parts and toss with the breadcrumbs, salt and pepper. Scoop this mixture onto each tomato. Lightly press down on the stuffing. Drizzle with the olive oil.

Place the tomatoes on a baking sheet and cook for about 20 minutes.

ƐNTERTAINING

Chicken Sate

Baked Fish with Mango, Ginger and Onion

Tomatoes and Mozzarella

Fettuccini with Calamari

Smoked Salmon in Cucumber Cups with Dill Vinaigrette

Scallops with Mustard Sauce

Cajun Shrimp Cocktail

Spaghetti with Garlic and Citrus

Quick Veal Piccatta

Hot Vinegar Shrimp

Salmon with Apple and Date Chutney

Couscous with Red Onions and Peas

Beef Wrapped Asparagus Spears

Penne with Asparagus, Smoked Salmon and Dill

Mushrooms in Garlic Sauce

White Bean and Sage Dip

Beef in Sherried Mushroom Sauce

Mexican Cinnamon Rice

Pork Chops with Garlic and Rosemary

Ginger and Onion Lobster

Corn with Red Bell Peppers and Green Onions

Pork Tenderloin with Orange-Pepper Sauce

Grilled Veal in Balsamic Pepper Sauce

Tangy Snow Peas

Chicken Sate

SERVES 8

THIS IS A QUICK VERSION of the Indonesian satay, a marvelously flavored street-vendor snack which is usually small, spicy meatballs skewered and barbecued, then served with a peanut sauce. Here, the peanut butter is incorporated into the marinade, so the longer the chicken is allowed to sit in the sauce, the more flavor it will absorb.

2   whole skinless boneless chicken breasts

2   tablespoons smooth peanut butter

1   tablespoon soy sauce

½   teaspoon hot pepper oil

1   tablespoon honey

1   tablespoon hot water

Cut the chicken breasts into 1-inch cubes and set aside. In a blender or food processor, puree the remaining ingredients. Remove to a medium bowl. Add the chicken and toss until it is coated with the sauce.

Place each piece of chicken on a rack placed over a baking sheet and broil, 3 inches from the flame, for 5 minutes. Turn the chicken over and cook for an additional 5 minutes.

Serve the chicken pieces on a platter with a small glass of toothpicks alongside for picking them up.

Tomatoes and Mozzarella

SERVES 10

MOZZARELLA USED TO BE MADE exclusively from buffalo's milk, but today is made from cow's milk. The mozzarella recommended in this recipe should be the freshest of cheeses, roughly ball-shaped and made in the traditional method, moist and dripping with whey.

4 small ripe tomatoes

2 to 4 fresh mozzarella cheese balls (bocconcini) depending on size

3 tablespoons extra-virgin olive oil

1 tablespoon fresh lemon juice

4 basil sprigs

Cut the tomatoes into slices. Cut the mozzarella into thin slices.

Arrange on a serving platter, alternating the tomatoes with the cheese. Mix together the oil and lemon juice. Pour the dressing over the mozzarella and tomatoes and garnish with the basil. Provide hors d'oeuvre plates and forks.

Smoked Salmon in Cucumber Cups with Dill Vinaigrette

MAKES 8

I LOVE SMOKED SALMON. I love dill. I love cucumbers. You could have predicted that this recipe would come along sooner or later. It's very quick to put together—no fancy ingredients, no culinary school techniques. But it's an elegant hors d'oeuvre that goes well with evening cocktails, or perhaps as a light appetizer before a main course.

1/8	pound smoked salmon
2	medium cucumbers
	Salt
2	tablespoons red wine vinegar
1	teaspoon dried dill
1/2	teaspoon Dijon-style mustard
	Salt and freshly ground pepper to taste
1/3	cup corn oil

Coarsely chop the salmon and set aside. Peel the cucumbers, trim off the ends and cut each one into 4 pieces. Scoop out some of the center seeds and allow to drain on paper towels. Sprinkle with salt.

In a small bowl, combine the vinegar, dill, mustard and a pinch of salt and pepper. Whisk together and very gradually add the corn oil in a thin stream. Pour the vinaigrette over the salmon and fold to combine.

Place about a teaspoon of the salmon into each cucumber cup.

Cajun Shrimp Cocktail

SERVES 4

MY COUSIN, SUE WILSON, moved from Delaware to Louisiana years ago and married into the Duhon clan, whose Cajun heritage goes back generations. If there's a cuisine that knows more about shrimp and spice than Cajun, I've yet to come across it. Here's a sauce from their world that trades the tangy bite of traditional cocktail sauces for the heat of the bayou. As the Duhons would say, "You may find like it, you."

½ cup low-fat mayonnaise

½ cup low-fat sour cream

1 tablespoon cider vinegar

1 teaspoon dry mustard

1 garlic clove, minced

½ teaspoon ground cumin

½ teaspoon cayenne pepper

½ teaspoon salt

2 tablespoons drained capers

2 tablespoons ketchup

1 tablespoon finely diced carrot

1 tablespoon finely diced celery

1 tablespoon finely diced green onion

Lemon wedges

20 shrimp, peeled, deveined, blanched

In a small bowl, whisk together all but the last 2 ingredients. Surround the bowl with lemon wedges and the shrimp.

Hot Vinegar Shrimp

LIKE SHRIMP? Like a little heat on your tongue? Like a little tangy bite around the edges? Then you're gonna love this dish. It's great for cocktail parties, sports gatherings, or setting out in the kitchen for your guests while you prepare the main meal.

Juice of ½ lemon, plus enough red wine vinegar to make ¼ cup

1 teaspoon soy sauce

1 tablespoon olive oil

1 pound medium shrimp, peeled, deveined

Salt to taste

Red pepper flakes to taste

⅓ cup chopped fresh cilantro

In a small bowl, combine the lemon juice mixture and the soy sauce.

Heat the oil in a sauté pan until hot but not smoking. Add the shrimp and sauté quickly, sprinkling with salt and red pepper flakes, about 1 minute on each side. Remove to a bowl.

Pour the lemon juice and soy mixture into the same sauté pan and cook about 2 minutes, reducing it by half. Add the shrimp and cook for another ½ minute. Swirl in the cilantro, remove to a serving plate and serve immediately with a small dish of toothpicks.

Beef Wrapped Asparagus Spears

MAKES ABOUT 12 PIECES

THIS IS A STAPLE OF THE hors d'oeuvre platters carried around by the waiters at posh affairs. Everyone always loves them, and you'll never have any leftovers. Oftentimes, however, the horseradish is left out, but I wouldn't recommend it. Nor would I use a "prepared horseradish sauce." Use pure, minced horseradish in a little vinegar—there are plenty of brands readily available in the supermarket.

3   to 4 asparagus spears, cut into
    2-inch pieces

3   to 4 roast beef slices, ⅛-inch
    thick

2   tablespoons horseradish
    Toothpicks

Bring a small pot of water to a boil. Blanch the asparagus in it for 3 minutes. Drain and rinse with cold water. Pat dry and set aside.

Cut the roast beef into 2 x 2½-inch squares. Smooth enough horseradish on each piece to just cover the topside. Place a spear of asparagus in the middle of each square and roll the beef around it. Secure with a toothpick, place on a platter and serve.

White Bean and Sage Dip

MAKES 2 CUPS

HUMMUS IS A MIDDLE EASTERN/Mediterranean hors d'oeuvre made from mashed chickpeas, tahini, garlic and lemon juice. While it's quite good, it usually tends toward the heavy side. Here's a light and fluffy version of hummus that you and your guests will find as satisfying as the original, but not nearly as weighty.

1 15-ounce can white Great Northern beans, drained

½ cup low-fat cottage cheese

2 tablespoons fresh lemon juice

1 tablespoon extra-virgin olive oil

2 garlic cloves, minced

1 teaspoon ground sage

1 tablespoon finely chopped fresh sage leaves

Salt and freshly ground pepper to taste

Put all of the ingredients except the sage leaves and salt and pepper into a blender or food processor. Puree until smooth. Stir in the sage leaves and adjust the taste with the salt and pepper.

Serve in a dish surrounded by raw vegetables and/or crackers.

Pork Chops with Garlic and Rosemary

SERVES 4

This is one of the simplest ways to enjoy a nice, thick, center-cut pork chop. The combination of garlic and rosemary is wonderful. I prefer to broil them standing on end, held by a beef rack set inside a broiling pan, which allows a lot of the rendered fat to drip away. Serve them garnished with a sprig of rosemary.

4   1-inch-thick center-cut pork chops
4   to 5 garlic cloves, sliced
    Olive oil
1   tablespoon crushed dried
    rosemary
    Rosemary sprigs for garnish

With a sharp knife, make several slits in each pork chop. Stuff slices of the garlic into each slit.

Rub the pork chops with the olive oil—not too heavily. Place on a preheated grill or broiler. Sprinkle with the rosemary.

Bake or grill until cooked through (about 5 minutes per side)—the meat should be 160°F in the center. Remove to a heated serving platter and serve.

Pork Tenderloin with Orange-Pepper Sauce

SERVES 4

POOR, OLD PORK HAS been trying for years to come out from under its bad reputation as a fat-laden meat best left to those without cholesterol worries. But while many cuts of pork are just that, pork tenderloin can be as clean and light as chicken breast, and, cooked just right, even more flavorful. And by adding a hint of citrus and the pungency of freshly cracked black pepper, you can make pork the star it's always wished to be.

16 ounces pork tenderloin, trimmed of fat and membrane

 3 tablespoons all-purpose flour

    Vegetable spray

⅓ cup chopped shallots

 1 teaspoon crushed black peppercorns

⅓ cup dry white wine

 1 tablespoon orange zest

⅔ cup orange juice

Cut the pork across the grain into ½-inch slices. Put the meat between 2 pieces of waxed paper and pound until it is ¼-inch thick. Dust lightly with flour after removing the paper.

Coat a wide, nonstick pan with vegetable spray. Heat the pan over medium-high heat and add the pork, being sure not to crowd the pan. Turn the meat once until it is golden brown on each side. Remove to a platter, cover and keep warm in a 200°F oven.

Add the shallots and pepper to the pan. Cook, stirring until the shallots are soft. Add the wine, orange zest and orange juice. Raise the heat to high and bring to a boil, stirring often. Cook until the sauce is reduced to half. Pour over the pork and serve.

Baked Fish with Mango, Ginger and Onion

SERVES 4

WHEN I WAS A STRUGGLING young musician years ago, dinner was dictated by dollars, not cuisine opportunities. But I was lucky at that time to have a good friend who taught me that few dollars doesn't equal mundane meals. Here's a perfect example of her point: inexpensive ingredients, very little time or talent needed, but a beautiful, gourmet result. Feel free to substitute peaches for the mango, or a red or Vidalia onion for the standard one.

Vegetable spray

1 pound white fish fillets (such as flounder, cod, scrod or halibut)

1 ½-inch piece gingerroot, peeled, sliced paper thin

1 small onion, thinly sliced into rings

1 medium mango, peeled, cut into slices

2 teaspoons chopped fresh thyme or ¼ teaspoon dried

Salt and freshly ground pepper to taste

Preheat the oven to 450°F.

If using a nonstick casserole, omit using the vegetable spray, if not, coat the bottom of the pot. Place the fish in the casserole in a single layer. Scatter the ginger and onion across the top of the fish. Scatter the mango around the pan. Top with the thyme, salt and pepper.

Bake the fish for about 10 minutes, or until the fish flakes easily. Place the fillets on serving plates, keeping the ginger and onion on top. Place the mango slices on top and around the fish on the plate. Pour the pan juices over the fish when serving.

Fettuccini with Calamari

SERVES 4

I CAME TO CALAMARI LATE in life. I just couldn't get the picture of a squid out of my head when offered the seafood delicacy, so I avoided it for almost four decades. My loss. Now enlightened, I never pass up an opportunity to enjoy it. Here's a marvelously simple way to do so and stay on the light side as well.

1   pound cleaned squid tubes (calamari)
    Vegetable spray
1   large red onion, thinly sliced,
    separated into rings
1   9-ounce package fresh fettuccini
3   large garlic cloves, minced
1   tablespoon lemon juice
¼   cup finely chopped fresh parsley
    Salt and freshly ground pepper to taste
    Lemon wedges for garnish

Cut the calamari crosswise into ½-inch-wide strips.

Coat a frying pan with vegetable spray and heat over a medium-high flame. Add the onion and cook, stirring often, until very soft but not brown—8 to 10 minutes.

Meanwhile, cook the fettuccini according to package instructions. It should be tender to the bite. Drain well.

To the onion, add the garlic and calamari. Cook, stirring constantly, until squid is opaque—2 to 3 minutes. Mix in the lemon juice. Add the fettuccini and half the parsley, mix gently, using 2 spoons, until heated through. Season with the salt and pepper. Sprinkle with remaining parsley and garnish with the lemon wedges.

Scallops with Mustard Sauce

SERVES 2

I LOVE SCALLOPS. Particularly the large sea scallops. They lend themselves so nicely to sauces and reductions, and are equally at home as an appetizer or an entrée. This is a very light, very easy recipe that allows you to play with it a little in your choice of mustard. I find a spicy, dark brown mustard works well. I would also suggest that you ask your seafood store for "dry" scallops, too—they are usually larger and have much better texture.

4	tablespoons water
2	teaspoons coarse grain brown mustard
1	teaspoon lemon juice
	Vegetable spray
1	small zucchini, biased-sliced ¼-inch thick
8	ounces fresh sea scallops
2	tablespoons cashews

Combine the water, mustard and lemon juice and set aside.

Coat a skillet with vegetable spray and heat over medium heat. Add the zucchini and cook, stirring, for 2 to 3 minutes or until tender. Remove the zucchini to a plate and keep warm.

Add the scallops to the pan and cook, turning them, until they are opaque. Add the sauce to the skillet and cook, stirring, until bubbly.

Place the scallop mixture on top of a layer of the zucchini, sprinkle with cashews and serve.

Spaghetti with Garlic and Citrus

SERVES 4

ONE OF THE EASIEST WAYS to lend a light, airy taste to any dish is to add citrus to it. The tangy sweetness of fruit and fruit juice always seems to lift a heavy dish while at the same time adding a bit of a surprise to each bite. Combine that lightness with my favorite herb—garlic—and you'll have a winner each time. Try this instead of a heavy tomato sauce one night, and feel free to add a few shrimp or maybe some calamari.

1 pound spaghetti

1 tablespoon olive oil

5 garlic cloves, thinly sliced

1 flat anchovy fillet

1 tablespoon lemon zest

¼ teaspoon red pepper flakes

3 tablespoons chopped fresh Italian parsley

2 tablespoons grated Parmesan cheese

Salt and freshly ground pepper to taste

Cook the spaghetti according to the package instructions, making sure the cooking water is salted. While the pasta is cooking, heat the oil in a 12-inch skillet over medium heat. Add the garlic and cook until it's golden. Remove the skillet from the heat and add the anchovy fillet, lemon zest, red pepper flakes and ½ cup of the pasta cooking water.

Reserve 1 cup of the pasta cooking water, then drain the pasta. Add the pasta to the lemon/garlic mix in the skillet and cook over medium-high heat, tossing the pasta and adding a little of the extra cooking water, if necessary.

Then add in the parsley, Parmesan and salt and pepper to taste. Toss well and serve.

Salmon with Apple and Date Chutney

SERVES 2

CHUTNEYS ARE ONE OF MY wife Toni's favorite things. While there are many different bottled varieties available in the markets, it's actually quite easy to make one fresh, and Toni's never made the same one twice. She particularly loves them with fish, and this is a quick and easy dish that I'm sure will show up on our table in the near future.

2   1-inch-thick salmon steaks
    Salt and freshly ground pepper to taste
2   teaspoons curry powder
⅔   cup chopped red onion
¾   cup chopped tart green apples
¼   cup chopped pitted dates
3   tablespoons apple juice
1   tablespoon white wine vinegar

Sprinkle each steak with salt and pepper and ¼ teaspoon of curry powder per side. Heat a large, nonstick skillet over medium heat and sauté the salmon for about 3 minutes on each side.

In another nonstick skillet, cook the onion over medium heat. When it begins to soften, add the apples, dates, apple juice and the remaining curry powder. Cook 2 minutes longer. Mix in the vinegar and simmer 1 minute longer. Season the curry to taste with salt and pepper. Transfer the salmon to plates and spoon the chutney alongside.

Penne with Asparagus, Smoked Salmon and Dill

SERVES 4

STEAMING IS ONE OF THE BEST ways to keep meals light and healthy while trying to come up with new ideas for dishes. Steaming locks in nutrients and cooks without any addition of oils or fats. If you have a large stockpot with a steamer insert, this dish takes no more time than putting the ingredients in the pot, turning on the heat and waiting a few minutes. So not only are you getting light and easy, you're not working for it.

1 pound penne

3 ounces (4 slices) smoked salmon, cut into 1½ x ¼-inch-thick strips

½ red onion, cut into rings

12 asparagus spears, trimmed, cut into 1½-inch lengths

Salt and freshly ground pepper to taste

2 tablespoons chopped fresh dill

On the bottom of a large steamer, pour boiling water. Return the water to a boil and add the penne.

Into the steamer basket, place the salmon, onion and asparagus. Place the pot over high heat and boil for 3 to 5 minutes. The boiling water cooking the pasta will steam the salmon. Remove the steamer basket and continue cooking the pasta.

When tender, drain the pasta and place in a serving bowl. Add the salmon and vegetables from the steamer basket. Adjust the flavor with salt and pepper and toss with the dill.

Beef in Sherried Mushroom Sauce

SERVES 2

SHALLOTS AND SHERRY are a masterful combination, and it's hard to go wrong with them as partners in a sauce. If you're looking to put a quick yet gourmet meal on the table, give this one a try. You'll get raves on the sauce, yet there's no fat in it (except for the beef). Can't get better than that.

2 1-inch-thick beef tenderloin steaks (about 5 ounces each)
   Salt and freshly ground pepper to taste
4 tablespoons minced shallots
6 ounces mushrooms, thinly sliced
4 tablespoons dry Sherry
1 tablespoon chopped fresh parsley

Season the steaks with salt and pepper. Heat a nonstick skillet over a medium-high flame and cook the steaks until desired doneness, about 4 minutes a side for medium-rare. Transfer the steaks to heated plates.

Add the shallots and mushrooms to the skillet and sauté until the mushrooms are softened, about 5 minutes. Add the Sherry and boil until the liquid is reduced slightly, about 2 minutes. Spoon the sauce over the steaks, sprinkle with parsley and serve.

Ginger and Onion Lobster

SERVES 5 TO 6

THERE'S SOMETHING ABOUT LOBSTER, isn't there? Something exotic, something indulgent, something almost sinful. Maybe that's why we love it. But while most of us would buy it in a restaurant, not many of us cook it at home, mainly because we have the mistaken impression that it's difficult to deal with, easily overcooked, and we're not sure what to do with it. Well, give this one a try—and see how easy it is to indulge yourself. The only downside is, it's so light there's nothing sinful about it. Guess you can't have everything.

1 tablespoon canola oil

2 pounds lobster meat, cut into large chunks

5 slices fresh gingerroot, julienned

4 green onions (green parts only), julienned lengthwise

1 red bell pepper, julienned lengthwise

½ teaspoon salt

½ cup seafood or chicken stock

2 tablespoons soy sauce

4 tablespoons rice wine or dry Sherry

1 teaspoon sesame oil

In a large skillet or wok, heat the canola oil over a high flame. When hot, add the lobster chunks and sauté for 2½ minutes. Remove the lobster and keep it warm.

To the skillet, add the ginger, green onions, red pepper and salt and sauté over medium heat for 1 minute. Add the stock, soy sauce and rice wine. Bring to a boil and reduce by half. Add the lobster meat, sprinkle in the sesame oil and toss well.

Grilled Veal in Balsamic Pepper Sauce

SERVES 4

BALSAMIC VINEGAR, like calamari, was another experience I put off until later in life, and now I can't get enough of it. It's completely replaced red wine vinegar in my cooking. I simply love the smokiness of it. In this dish, we combine that smokey flavor with the pop of freshly cracked pepper and let the two of them work their magic on some veal. You could just as easily substitute chicken or pork for the veal and get the same fabulous results.

4   2-inch-thick veal loin chops

½   teaspoon kosher salt

½   teaspoon freshly ground pepper
    Vegetable spray

1   tablespoon olive oil

2¼ teaspoons balsamic vinegar

2   tablespoons coarsely chopped fresh parsley

2   lemons, halved, seeded

Preheat a grill or broiler until it is very hot.

Sprinkle the veal with half of the salt and pepper. Coat the grill or broiling pan with vegetable spray and grill the chops for 10 minutes per side.

While the chops are cooking, combine the remaining salt and pepper, the olive oil and balsamic vinegar in a jar. Cover tightly and shake well.

Place the veal on a serving platter and drizzle the oil mixture over it. Sprinkle with the parsley and serve with the lemon halves.

Quick Veal Piccatta

SERVES 2

THE NAME OF THIS DISH is a little redundant. I've always found piccatta to be very quick and easy to make. I've also loved its lightness, which the wine and lemon contribute to nicely. And while you're saving time putting this gourmet dish on the table, keep in mind that the light sauce lends itself wonderfully to chicken or white fish as well. Enjoy experimenting with it.

½ pound veal scaloppine, cut into ¼-inch slices

Flour for dredging

Salt and freshly ground pepper to taste

2 tablespoons dry white wine

2 tablespoons lemon juice

2 thin lemon slices

2 teaspoons finely chopped fresh parsley

Place the veal between 2 pieces of waxed paper and pound them with a mallet to no thinner than ⅛ inch.

Blend the flour with the salt and pepper, then dip the meat in the mixture to coat lightly.

Heat a nonstick skillet over medium-high heat and add the veal. Cook the veal for 2 minutes on each side and then remove it to a warm plate. Add the wine and lemon juice and bring to a boil. Return the veal to the pan and coat it with the sauce. Serve immediately garnished with the lemon slices and parsley.

Couscous with Red Onions and Peas

SERVES 4

COUSCOUS IS A GREAT ALTERNATIVE to potatoes or rice. I like the color combination of red onions and peas, but feel free to toss in any diced vegetable you like—perhaps a mix of bell pepper, or even currants, chopped nuts or bits of fresh fruit.

1	tablespoon extra-virgin olive oil
1	cup diced red onions
1	cup fresh or frozen green peas
½	teaspoon ground cumin
½	teaspoon salt
1	cup water
1	cup couscous

In a heavy skillet, heat the olive oil and onions. Sauté over medium heat until the onions are translucent. Add the peas, cumin, salt, water and couscous. Bring to a simmer. Cover and remove from heat. Let stand for 5 minutes or until all of the water is absorbed and the peas are bright green.

Mushrooms in Garlic Sauce

SERVES 6

THIS IS A QUICK, LIGHT and very versatile dish. It can stand alone as a side dish, or my wife Toni and I have used it as a sauce on breaded turkey cutlets sautéed in a little olive oil. It has a big, gourmet taste, but takes almost no time to make and is light in calories and fat.

1 teaspoon olive oil

½ pound mushrooms, stems trimmed, brushed clean, quartered

4 garlic cloves, thinly sliced

2 teaspoons fresh lemon juice

2 tablespoons dry Sherry

2 tablespoons chicken broth

2 tablespoons beef broth

½ teaspoon paprika

¼ teaspoon crushed red pepper

Salt and freshly ground pepper to taste

1 tablespoon minced fresh parsley

Heat the oil in a skillet until very hot and add the mushrooms and garlic. Sauté for 2 minutes, lower the heat and add the lemon juice, Sherry, both broths, paprika, red pepper, salt and pepper. Simmer a minute or 2 more. Sprinkle with parsley and serve.

Mexican Cinnamon Rice

SERVES 4

I CAME BY THIS DISH through my brother-in-law, Ken Morris. At home, you'll usually find him cooking Mexican. The cinnamon and currants in this dish add a festive sweetness to the rice.

Vegetable spray

½ cup chopped onion

1 garlic clove, minced

2 teaspoons ground cinnamon

1 cup uncooked long-grain rice

¼ cup currants

2¼ cups chicken stock

½ teaspoon salt

1 teaspoon chopped fresh cilantro

Coat the bottom of a nonstick saucepot with vegetable spray. Sauté the onion, garlic and cinnamon over medium heat until the onion is soft. Stir in the remaining ingredients except for the cilantro. Bring to a boil over high heat, lower the heat, cover and simmer for 18 minutes. Fluff the rice, stir in the cilantro and serve.

Corn with Red Bell Peppers and Green Onions

SERVES 5

Vegetable spray

1 large red bell pepper, seeded, chopped into ¼-inch pieces

16 ounces frozen corn kernels, thawed

2 teaspoons minced fresh thyme or 1 teaspoon dried

½ bunch green onions

Salt and freshly ground pepper to taste

IT'S ALWAYS NICE to add color to a plate. And a side dish is a perfect place to do it. The bright yellow, red and green of this dish will add visual punch to your presentation, and the subtle combination of flavors works as nicely on the palate. A great one for those with little time.

Coat a skillet with vegetable spray and heat over a medium-high flame. Add the red pepper and sauté until it is tender. Add the corn and thyme and cook for 4 minutes more. Add the green onions and cook until they are slightly wilted. Season with salt and pepper to taste.

Tangy Snow Peas

SERVES 4

ALAS. THE LOWLY SNOW PEA. Beautiful, different, crispy. But kind of bland. So dress it up. A little sugar, garlic and vinegar, and before you know it, a star has emerged from the chorus line. Great with fish and chicken, or cooled on a salad.

Vegetable spray

1 garlic clove, chopped

10 to 12 ounces snow peas, strings removed

1 teaspoon sugar

1 teaspoon apple cider vinegar

1 teaspoon cornstarch, dissolved in 1 tablespoon water

Salt to taste

Coat a wide skillet or wok with vegetable spray. Add the garlic and snow peas and cook over high heat for a minute or 2. Sprinkle in the sugar, vinegar and the dissolved cornstarch. Sprinkle with the salt, stir to blend, cover and steam for 30 seconds.

DESSERTS

Spicy Oatmeal Cookies

Vanilla Custard with
   Nectarine Sauce

Chocolate Pudding

Spiced Peach Crumble

Sherried Pears

Baked Bananas with Coconut

Baked Cinnamon Apples

Russian Apricot Pudding

Bananas Foster

Hot Fruit Compote

Creamy Lemon Pie

Spicy Oatmeal Cookies

MAKES 6 LARGE COOKIES

MAKING A COOKIE THAT IS LIGHT, easy, low in fat and yet tasty sounds akin to creating a car that uses water for fuel. But you can do it. These are chewy, filling cookies that are terrific served with frozen yogurt or a cup of afternoon Earl Grey tea. If you really want to give the kids a treat, wrap them in waxed paper and put them in the freezer. They make a great "emergency" dessert.

Vegetable spray

¼ cup low-fat vanilla yogurt

¼ cup canola oil

½ cup maple syrup

1 cup rolled oats

½ cup whole wheat flour

1 teaspoon baking powder

½ teaspoon ground cardamom

¼ teaspoon ground mace

½ teaspoon salt

½ cup raisins

Preheat the oven to 375°F.

Coat 3 cookie sheets with vegetable spray.

In a large bowl, mix together the yogurt, oil and syrup. Stir in the oats.

Sift together the dry ingredients and stir into the wet mixture. Add the raisins and combine. Divide the batter by 6 and place 2 portions on each cookie sheet. Smooth out the batter so that it is circular and bake for 20 minutes.

Cool on a wire rack.

Vanilla Custard with Nectarine Sauce

SERVES 2

Here's something that usually comes laden with fat, calories and cholesterol. But this faux custard tastes fabulous and is great for those times when a creamy dessert is craved, but the fat that usually accompanies it is not. Try a dollop on top of fresh fruit, or a low-calorie cookie (like the Spicy Oatmeal Cookies on page 114), or on a baked apple.

CUSTARD

- 1 cup low-fat cottage cheese
- 1 cup low-fat ricotta cheese
- 1 cup low-fat vanilla yogurt
- ⅓ cup honey
- 1 teaspoon vanilla extract

SAUCE

- 1 5½-ounce can peach nectar
- 1 tablespoon cornstarch
- 2 teaspoons water
- 1 teaspoon minced crystallized gingerroot
- ½ teaspoon lemon zest
- ¼ teaspoon lemon juice
- ⅛ teaspoon vanilla extract
- 1 unpeeled nectarine, sliced

FOR CUSTARD: Place the cottage cheese and ricotta in a blender or food processor. Blend until they are smooth. With the motor running, add the remaining ingredients and process until well mixed.

FOR SAUCE: In a small saucepot, heat the peach nectar. In a small cup, blend the cornstarch with the water until smooth. Add to the peach nectar, stirring constantly. Simmer until thickened. Remove from the heat and stir in the gingerroot, lemon zest, lemon juice and vanilla extract. Cool the mixture for 5 minutes. Stir the sliced nectarines into the sauce. Spoon the vanilla custard onto dessert plates. Pour the sauce over the custard.

Chocolate Pudding

OH, THAT I COULD HAVE HAD this recipe when I was growing up! A quick, simple way to make my own chocolate pudding! Well, better late than never, right? This one's for those of us still hooked on pudding and rich chocolate flavor, but needing a lighter variety. And the kids will love it, as well.

1   pound low-fat ricotta cheese

¼   cup chocolate syrup

¼   teaspoon almond extract

2   tablespoons sugar

Place the ricotta in a fine sieve and allow it to drain for up to 30 minutes.

Place the drained ricotta and the remaining ingredients in a blender or food processor and pulse until the mixture is very smooth. Divide into dessert cups and chill.

Spiced Peach Crumble

SERVES 4

DESSERTS OFTEN TAKE MOST of our time in the kitchen, especially if our desire is to put a mouth-watering, enticing, intoxicating one on the table. For the little work it takes, this peach crumble delivers all of that and more. Use fresh peaches only if they are truly ripe and in season, otherwise, frozen will do. Serve this dessert warm with some low-fat vanilla frozen yogurt, or topped with a dollop of low-fat sour cream.

1   pound frozen peaches

2   tablespoons maple syrup

½   teaspoon ground mace

1   tablespoon lemon juice

½   cup crumbled gingersnaps

Preheat the oven to 425°F.

Spread the peaches in an 8-inch ovenproof dish. Mix together the maple syrup, mace and lemon juice and drizzle it over the peaches. Sprinkle the cookie crumbs over the top and bake for 20 minutes.

Sherried Pears

SERVES 6

THERE ARE SOME DESSERTS we see on the dessert cart in those fancy restaurants that we're sure—absolutely positive—that we could never make at home. Surprise. If you can bring liquid to a boil, you can make this exceptional dessert.

⅔ cup packed light brown sugar

½ cup cream Sherry

2 tablespoons lemon juice

1 teaspoon ground cinnamon

½ cup water

6 medium pears, sliced ¼-inch thick

In a small skillet, combine the brown sugar, Sherry, lemon juice, cinnamon and water. Cook, stirring, over medium heat until the mixture is smooth and beginning to bubble. Add the pears and cook until they are heated all the way through. Remove the pears to a serving dish and raise the heat to high, reducing the sauce a little. Pour over the pears and serve.

Baked Bananas with Coconut

SERVES 4

HERE'S ONE THE KIDS will absolutely adore—rich with natural sweetness. Watch it closely in the oven, so you can get the coconut browned just as the brown sugar caramelizes.

5 medium bananas

Vegetable spray

⅓ cup orange juice

1 tablespoon lemon juice

1 tablespoon packed brown sugar

⅔ cup shredded coconut

Preheat the oven to 375°F. Cut the bananas crosswise into halves, then cut each half lengthwise into halves. Coat a 9-inch pie plate or baking dish with vegetable spray. Place the bananas in it and drizzle with the orange and lemon juices. Sprinkle with the brown sugar and coconut. Bake for 8 to 10 minutes, until the coconut is golden.

Baked Cinnamon Apples

SERVES 6

THIS IS A FALL CLASSIC that can be enjoyed year 'round. The raisins and maple syrup replace the refined sugars, so you get the sweetness without the downside. Kids will think they're getting a special treat, while you're getting something good into them. The cinnamon stick poking out from each apple gives them a whimsical air. Serve it with vanilla frozen yogurt or topped with Vanilla Custard (see page 115).

6	large firm apples
⅓	cup raisins
¼	cup finely chopped walnuts
6	cinnamon sticks
½	cup frozen apple juice concentrate
¼	cup maple syrup
½	cup water
¼	teaspoon ground mace
¼	teaspoon ground cloves
1	teaspoon sugar

Preheat the oven to 375°F.

Core the apples. Place them in a shallow baking dish. Mix together the raisins and walnuts. Fill each apple with a cinnamon stick and the raisin and nut mixture.

Combine the apple juice concentrate, maple syrup and water. Pour the mixture over the apples. There should be about ½ inch of water on the bottom of the pan.

Mix together the spices and sugar. Sprinkle the mixture over the apples. Cover the pan with foil and bake for 20 minutes. Remove the apples to serving plates and pour the juices over each apple just before serving.

Russian Apricot Pudding

MAKES ABOUT 1½ CUPS

ORIGINALLY, A PUDDING was a sausage, or anything cooked inside a bag or cloth—usually meats. This was back in the 1400s. It wasn't until the early twentieth century that it came to mean something sweet served after dinner. While I can't attest to the authenticity of its Russian heritage, I can tell you that this is a rich, fruity pudding that goes well with spiced cookies or a cup of cappuccino.

2 cups water

1 cup (about 6 ounces) dried apricot halves

¼ cup sugar

3 tablespoons cornstarch

Dash salt

In a small saucepot, heat the water and apricots to a boil. Reduce heat. Cover and simmer until tender, about 15 minutes. Reserve the cooking liquid. Place the apricots and ½ cup cooking liquid into a blender. Cover and puree until a uniform consistency is reached. Press the puree through a sieve.

Mix the sugar, cornstarch and salt in a 1½-quart saucepot. Gradually stir in the apricot puree and remaining cooking liquid. Heat to boiling over medium heat, stirring constantly. Boil and stir for 1 minute.

Pour into dessert dishes. Serve warm, with a dollop of low-fat sour cream.

Bananas Foster

SERVES 4

A CLASSIC...AND A DISH that impresses anyone. It was created at Antoine's, in the French Quarter of New Orleans. While it's actually quite easy to make, you have to be careful, especially when igniting the liqueurs. But the results are impressive, both visually and on the palate.

2 tablespoons light brown sugar

1 teaspoon ground cinnamon

½ cup banana liqueur

½ cup dark rum

4 bananas, halved lengthwise

Mint sprigs for garnish

In a small bowl, combine the brown sugar and cinnamon with a fork. In a heavy skillet, over medium heat, stir the sugar and cinnamon until the sugar begins to melt. Pour in the banana liqueur and ¼ cup dark rum. Cook and stir until the mixture becomes thick and syrupy, about 5 minutes. Add the bananas and lightly coat them with the syrup. Add the remaining ¼ cup of rum. Swirl the pan and ignite the rum carefully. Quickly swirl the pan, then set the pan down and baste the bananas with the sauce until the flame goes out.

Remove the skillet from the heat. Place the banana slices on each plate, side by side. Drizzle with the sauce from the pan. Decorate with the mint.

Hot Fruit Compote

MOM WAS A LOVER OF ICE CREAM. But she would never eat it "naked," as she put it. She always had to put something on it. Hot fudge was, of course, her topping of choice, but every once in a while she'd put together this compote and top her vanilla ice cream with it (it always had to be vanilla). It's best if it's served warm on the ice cream, but you'll have to eat it fast that way. It's also not a bad dessert all by itself. If the fruits are out of season, feel free to use canned—just drain and rinse the sugar syrup off of them first.

2 tablespoons flour

½ cup brown sugar

8 tablespoons unsalted butter

1 cup Sherry

1½ to 2 cups pineapple chunks

1½ to 2 cups chunked ripe pears

1½ to 2 cups chunked ripe peaches

½ to 1 cup diced prunes or cherries (optional)

Combine the flour, brown sugar, butter and Sherry in a saucepan and cook slowly over low heat, stirring constantly, until the mixture is thick and smooth.

Arrange the fruit in a 9 x 12-inch glass casserole dish and pour the sauce mixture over it. Let the compote stand overnight. When ready to serve, bake at 350°F for 15 to 20 minutes, then serve warm.

Creamy Lemon Pie

SERVES 6 TO 8

MY FAMILY LOVED PIE. One of my earliest memories was my grandmother—we called her "Mamaw"—carrying her famous apple pie into the dining room in her house in Charleston, West Virginia. The smell was incredible, and set my nose for pie for the rest of my life. This is a recipe I found in my grandmother's cookbook. It's light and easy to make, and has a tang you'll not soon forget.

10 squares low-fat graham crackers

1 teaspoon unsalted butter, melted

1 egg white

3 egg yolks

1 14-ounce can nonfat sweetened condensed milk

½ cup lemonade concentrate

½ cup heavy cream

1 teaspoon sugar

⅛ cup nonfat cottage cheese

Preheat the oven to 350°F.

Place the graham cracker squares in the bowl of a food processor and pulse until they become crumbs. With the motor running, add the melted butter and egg white. Scrape the mixture into a 9-inch pie pan and press it into the bottom and sides of the pan. It will be sticky. Bake the crust in the oven for 15 minutes. Remove from the oven and allow to cool on a wire rack.

In a medium mixing bowl, beat the egg yolks until they are frothy. Add the condensed milk and the lemonade concentrate. Pour this mixture into the crust and refrigerate .

While the pie is chilling, pour the heavy cream and sugar into a small bowl. Beat with a wire whisk until it forms soft peaks. Using a fine sieve and a spoon, press the cottage cheese through and into the whipped cream. Fold to combine and spread over the pie. Chill for an additional ½ hour.

Index